WITHDRAWN

PROPERTY OF:
DAVID O. McKAY LIBRARY
BYU-IDAHO
REXBURG ID 83460-0405
DAVID O. McKAY LIBRARY
BYU-

MAR 2 8 2024

P9-ELG-358

3 1404 00830 1274

OCT 2 6 2008

Other titles

Pigs Do Fly
Terry Denton
PICTURES BY Terry Denton

Crime Doesn't Pay
Beverley MacDonald
CARTOONS BY Andrew Weldon

We Came From Slime
Ken McNamara
PICTURES BY Andrew Plant

There Are Bugs in Your Bed
Heather Catchpole and Vanessa Woods
PICTURES BY Craig Smith

Hauntings Happen and Ghosts Get Grumpy
Meredith Costain
PICTURES BY Craig Smith

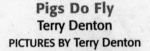

www.annickpress.com/microsites/itstrue.html

Diana Lawrenson   PICTURES BY Leigh Hobbs

IT'S TRUE!

Your Hair Is Dead

annick press
toronto + new york + vancouver

Copyright © text Diana Lawrenson 2006
Copyright © illustrations Leigh Hobbs 2006
Series design copyright © Ruth Grüner 2006

Annick Press Ltd.
First published in Australia by Allen & Unwin.

All rights reserved. No part of this work covered by the copyrights
hereon may be reproduced or used in any form or by any means—
graphic, electronic, or mechanical—without prior written
permission of the publisher.

Proofread by Helen Godolphin
Production of this edition by Antonia Banyard
Cover photograph: Gail Shumway/Getty Images
Set in 12.5pt Minion by Ruth Grüner

Cataloging in Publication
Lawrenson, Diana
It's true! your hair is dead / Diana Lawrenson ; pictures by Leigh Hobbs.

Includes index.
First published in Australia under title: It's true! your hair grows 15
kilometres a year.
ISBN-13: 978-1-55451-024-5 (bound)
ISBN-10: 1-55451-024-4 (bound)
ISBN-13: 978-1-55451-023-8 (pbk.)
ISBN-10: 1-55451-023-6 (pbk.)

1. Hair—Juvenile literature. I. Lawrenson, Diana. It's true! Your hair
grows 15 kilometres a year. II. Title.

QM488.L39 2006   j612.7'99   C2006-901256-3

Printed in Canada

1 3 5 7 9 10 8 6 4 2

Published in the U.S.A. by
Annick Press (U.S.) Ltd.

Distributed in Canada by:
Firefly Books Ltd.
66 Leek Crescent
Richmond Hill, ON
L4B 1H1

Distributed in the U.S.A. by:
Firefly Books (U.S.) Inc.
P.O. Box 1338
Ellicott Station
Buffalo, NY 14205

Visit our website at: www.annickpress.com

Contents

WHY HAIR?

Why Hair?

I grew up hating my hair, so it seems odd that I've written a book about it. But when the idea dropped into my mind, it set dozens of thoughts exploding in all directions. I thought about babies and barbers and balding, and before long I had dozens of questions. Did stone-age men shave? Why do we need eyelashes? Is it true that Egyptian queens wore beards? Does your hair really keep growing after you're dead?

I spent a lot of time asking people questions, reading books and trawling the Internet. Hair turned up everywhere—in musicals, fairytales and old sayings, in books about inventions, on websites about crime-solving methods. Some discoveries made me laugh, some were disgusting, and some made my hair stand on end. Mostly they gave me a huge buzz. I hope you'll find the same.

Diana Lawrenson

Chapter 1

Secrets in hair

A single strand of your hair can tell people about you, even if you're miles away from it, or dead. It reveals the major racial group you belong to. It can show if you've been poisoned or taking certain drugs. It may help prove you innocent or guilty of a crime.

Hair takes longer to rot than the fleshy parts of a body. If a body is frozen, or buried in a hot, dry place, hair can last for thousands of years. The Ice Man[1] of the European Alps, Egyptian mummies and frozen mammoths still had hair when they were discovered.

[1] A Neolithic man froze to death 5300 years ago in the European Alps. Hikers discovered him as an ice mummy when the snow melted during the unusually warm summer of 1991.

Hair and crime

Hair holds many clues that scientists can uncover.

Poisons such as arsenic, mercury and lead, and drugs such as cocaine, heroin and marijuana can stay in hair for days, or years. Forensic scientists are able to separate them through chemical tests.

At a crime scene, hair is valuable trace evidence. It's collected by forceps or a sticky tape or a filter vacuum and taken back to the laboratory. Scientists who look at it under a microscope can work out what part of the body it's from, whether it belongs to a young child or an adult, and if it is dyed. The type of dye can be determined, too.

A forensic scientist can see if a strand belongs to a person or a dog, or other animal.

If a hair from a crime scene matches another (e.g., one from a person's hairbrush), it can identify a missing person, or a victim, or a suspect in a crime.

Hair pulled out during a violent struggle can be enough to solve a crime—a crime a criminal thought he'd planned perfectly. This is because the hair that tells the most about you is a strand that's been plucked or yanked out, rather than one that's been shed naturally, or cut off.

Plucked hair has the root and some skin cells attached to it. The DNA on a microscopic piece of tissue attached to the root of one of our hairs is enough to identify and set us apart from anybody else in the world, unless we have an identical twin. It even shows if we are male or female.

Hair collects evidence too. In many countries, fine hair brushes are dusted over imported fruit. The brushes are then examined under microscopes to see if the fruit carries any foreign mites that could damage crops.

Mementoes and murder

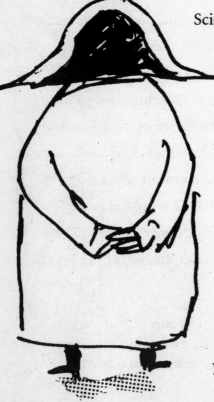

Scientific examination of hair has helped uncover how Napoleon Bonaparte, the Emperor of France, really died in 1821. Back then his doctors believed his death was due to cancer of the stomach. But it wasn't . . .

From 1815 the English held Napoleon prisoner on the island of St. Helena. During these years, his valet kept a diary.

When it was published 50 years ago, Swedish scientist Dr. Sten Forshufvud read the descriptions of Napoleon and his many ailments. Over time Napoleon's thirst had increased, he'd lost a lot of body hair and he became very fat—three of the many symptoms of arsenic poisoning. Had Napoleon been murdered?

The one way to find out if these suspicions were correct was to examine the Emperor's hair.

In the days before photographs, people gave away hair as a keepsake to friends or lovers, to be woven into a ring or bracelet or put in a locket. Napoleon did this, too (and people even souvenired some from his corpse!). Around 150 years after he died, forensic scientists tested strands of his hair and were able to show they *did* contain a large amount of arsenic.

Who gave it to Napoleon, and why? Canadian historian Dr. Ben Weider helped provide the answers.[2]

Napoleon had many enemies, including the French

[2] See page 85 for the books by Dr. Weider and Dr. Forshufvud that explain how they gathered the evidence. Most people accept their conclusion that Napoleon was murdered.

royal family. One of his staff, the Count de Monthelon, was a secret royalist, and he was responsible for Napoleon's wine on St. Helena. He was able to add tiny amounts of arsenic to the wine casks—enough to make Napoleon seriously sick, but not enough to kill him.

There's an extra twist to the story. The valet's diaries record that a few days before the end, an unknown person (now thought to be the Count) gave Napoleon medicines for two of his arsenic-induced complaints: constipation and terrible thirst. One medicine was an overdose of calomel, and the other was a drink of orange and oil of bitter almonds. These two concoctions combine in the stomach to form mercury cyanide—a deadly poison. That is what finally killed Napoleon Bonaparte.

Chapter 2

Fine? Frizzy? Fair?

Do you ever moan about your hair being too curly or too frizzy or too straight? So did people who lived thousands of years ago. They crimped and curled and colored their hair *and* their beards. Perhaps you're glad you have blond hair. You wouldn't have been if the

Romans had captured you. They would have cut it off to make a wig. And made you a slave.

Your hair depends a lot on the genes that you inherit from your parents. If you have Asian parents your hair will be straight and black. If you're Caucasian ("white" people from Europe, western Asia and parts of India and North Africa) you'll have wavy blond, brown or red hair. If you come from Africa or parts of the Pacific, your head will be covered in tight black or brown curls. And if you have mixed ancestry, who knows what you'll end up with?

Asian hair strands are the thickest of all. Amongst Caucasians, red strands are the coarsest and blond strands the finest.

Follicle follies

Hair grows up from tiny dents in the skin called follicles. These follicles are like microscopic socks that extend down through the layers of skin and into the layer of fat and tiny blood vessels below. We each have about five million (5,000,000) hair follicles on our body.

Follicles determine the type of hair you have. Round, straight follicles make hair straight; oval, kinked follicles make it wavy; and flattened, curly follicles make it curl.

You can change your hair from straight to curly or vice versa, but the change will always be temporary. You'll go back to your natural state after a few days if you've used mousse or spray, or after some months if you've had a perm. The new hair emerging

from each follicle will be unaffected by the perm and will grow in its natural shape.

A tiny gland that opens into each follicle produces oil that lubricates the hair and surrounding skin. It keeps the hair supple and prevents the skin from drying out.

Color me in

Cells in the follicles produce a coloring—a pigment—called melanin, and there are two forms of it. Eumelanin makes hair black or brown, while pheomelanin makes it blond or shades of red.

If there is no melanin, or if it's not properly transferred to skin, hair and eyes, the person will have a condition called albinism. Many albinos have very pale skin and some have white or whitish-yellow hair. Some, but not all, have pink-red eyes.

Albinism spells trouble for animals. It's so easy for predators to see them.

White squirrels are said to be good luck. The largest colony of albino squirrels lives in Olney, Illinois.

Graying gracefully

Hair turns "gray" gradually when the follicles stop producing pigment one by one over many years. The first gray strands often appear when a person is in their twenties. While some pigment is left in a strand of hair, both its normal color and white can be seen along its length. When no pigment at all is in the individual hair, it is white. But when white or partially white hairs lie beside dark or red ones, the eye sees them as gray, even though they're not *really* gray. Eventually, when none of the strands has any pigment, the entire head of hair is white.

Beards and moustaches often turn gray before the hair on the scalp does.

Gray for the guillotine

There's a story that Marie Antoinette, the last queen of France, turned gray overnight before she was put to death. Some people believe it's much more likely the imprisoned queen developed a balding condition triggered by severe stress. (Who wouldn't be stressed when they are locked up and expecting to have their head chopped off?) This can cause pigmented hair to fall out suddenly, over just a few days, leaving the person with only gray-white hair.

Flaming nonsense

It's a myth that people with red hair are more hot-tempered than others. Wouldn't you be fed up if you had to listen to comments about the color of your hair from the time you were tiny?

12

Who wouldn't feel like blowing their top when someone says, "Temper, temper, Carrottop (or Ginger)"?

Even if parents don't have red hair themselves, they may carry the gene for it. Both parents must carry the gene for one of their children to be a redhead.

Dyeing to be different

Henna is a reddish dye that has been found on the hair of Egyptian mummies. It comes from the leaves of a plant called the Egyptian privet. Men as well as women used it, and even dyed their beards with it. It's still used today.

Women have bleached their hair since Roman times. Back then they used a mixture of wood ash, lime and sodium bicarbonate. Centuries later, women mixed saltpeter (potassium nitrate, which is used in gunpowder, fertilizers and preservatives) with borax to bleach hair; they applied leeches soaked in vinegar to blacken hair; and they boiled animal blood blended with oil to obliterate gray hair. Disgusting!

Today dyes can be temporary, semipermanent or permanent. Simple temporary dyes are often made from walnut shells, chamomile flowers or the golden stigmas from crocus blooms. These plant infusions enhance rather than change the color of a person's hair, and they wash out easily.

Semipermanent dyes will last for about half a dozen shampoos. "Permanent" ones don't wash out —but they do grow out as new growth emerges in its natural color from the scalp. The color change is only permanent on the hair that's treated.

Some dyes need to be skin-tested before use to make sure the person is not allergic to them.

Wear and scare

Want to match your football team's colors? These days you can, by spraying your hair with dye from cans. But you might make Great Aunt Gertrude's hair stand on end—a scary sight.[3] Your old aunt will see the bright colors last only until your next hair wash, although it's a topic she's sure to raise for a long time afterwards.

[3] This reaction to shock is the same that occurs when animals are cold or angry. See how it happens on pages 34–35 in "Ghosts, growls and goose-bumps."

Shave for a cure

Would you shave your head to raise money? Lots of people do. From Kentucky to Wellington, Ottawa to Australia, people cut their hair to raise money for people with cancer, leukemia and other life-threatening diseases. If your hair is long enough, it can be used to make wigs for children with cancer. Or if you love your locks too much to lose them, you can dye them blue instead, as a fundraiser.

Chapter 3

Hair is (almost) everywhere

You may not think it, but we're hairy all over. The only external parts of human bodies that are *really* bare are the lips, the soles of our feet and the palms of our hands. Have a look through a magnifying glass.

Hair starts growing over babies several months before they're born. This first hair is called lanugo (lan-OO-go). It's short, silky and colorless. You can see it clearly on tiny babies born prematurely.

Normally, lanugo is shed in the last weeks before the baby is born. It's replaced by coarser, colored hair on the head, eyebrows and eyelids. Short, fine, almost invisible hair called vellus replaces the lanugo on the baby's face and body. You can just see vellus hair on boys and girls who haven't reached puberty, and on women's faces. It's a fine fuzz a bit like the skin of a peach.

At puberty, coarse, colored hair grows in the armpits and pubic areas, on arms and legs, and on boys' chests. This is called terminal hair. When they are middle-aged, men start growing hair in their ears.

Whiskers, manes and tails

There are mammals that look hairless, but they're not. Some whales, such as the humpback, have a few strands on the top of their heads. Dolphins are born with hairs along the top of their beaks. These disappear after a few weeks, but while a calf is tiny the hairs help it find and stimulate the mother's internal nipple for suckling.

When hair grows thickly all over an animal it's called fur. Like humans, animals' hair grows unevenly: a lion has a mane around its neck, a horse has a long switch on its tail, and most animals have whiskers beside their noses and mouths. Some have whiskers growing from their eyebrows, too.

Although each strand of hair is extremely thin, it's very tough. It's made of a substance called keratin that also forms our fingernails and toenails, as well as claws, hooves, pig bristles, bird feathers, horns, and the spiny quills of porcupines and hedgehogs.

Lions' manes protect their necks from injury when they fight each other over lionesses. Animal whiskers grow from nerve-rich areas and are acutely sensitive to tiny movements in the air indicating nearby danger or prey. In murky water a seal's whiskers help it find food. Horses use their tails to brush off flies. But what does hair on humans do?

The hair on our heads

Imagine being bald. Whenever you brushed past an overhanging thorny branch or bumped your head ... ouch! There's practically no padding between our skin and our skull, so it's just as well we have hair on our scalps that protects us from minor injuries.

Hair protects our scalps from sunburn that may lead to skin cancers, and it also keeps our heads warm. We lose a lot of body heat from our heads, especially babies, as they don't have much hair. It's important for them to wear caps or hats in cold weather. Sailors and skiers should wear hats too, especially if they are bald.

Eyebrows channel droplets away from the eyes. Think of early humans hunting on hot days in Africa, stalking animals or running full tilt. If sweat got into their eyes their vision would blur and they might lose sight of their prey altogether.

Eyelashes protect our eyes from dust and granules blown by the wind.

The hair in our **nostrils** traps dust and stops it from entering our lungs.

Pubic hair and underarm hair

This hair first grows when boys and girls reach puberty. Nobody is quite sure why we have it.

It's possible that the hair under the arms provides a larger surface for sweat to evaporate from.

Growing and going

If you have your hair cut every few weeks, you probably assume your hair is always growing. It's not. What's more, it doesn't even grow at the same rate all over. If it did, some of us might be trimming, shaving, plucking, sugaring or waxing some part of ourselves the whole time.

Our hairs cycle through several phases, and at any one time we have hair in all of these phases:

> **anagen**, the growing phase
>
> **catagen**, the breaking-down phase
>
> **telogen**, the resting phase
>
> **exogen**, the shedding phase.

On the scalp about 85 percent of hairs are in the growing phase at the same time, but in the eyebrows only 50 percent are. If all the strands were synchronized in the same phase at exactly the same time, we'd have periods of being eyebrow-less or eyelash-less or completely bald.

Scalp hair grows the fastest and has the longest life cycle (several years). Our eyelashes, eyebrows, and the hair on our arms, legs and body, have much shorter life cycles that last between three and eighteen months. The hairs there spend different lengths of time in each phase, too.

Next time an eyelash pokes painfully in your eye instead of falling out and blowing away, remember it's just finished its life cycle. A new one, firmly fixed for the time being, is growing to take its place.

The genes we inherit and our
hormones control the length
and rate hair grows on
different parts of our
body, so we're all
different. Men grow beards

and women don't. Some men are hairy-chested while
others have only a few strands on their torso.

Drop from the top

Every day we painlessly lose 30 to 100 hairs from our
scalp. You see them on your hairbrush, your shoulders,
or tangled in the drain when you've washed your hair.
The tiny, whitish root is often visible on the end
of a strand. These hairs are several years old. Here's
how it works . . .

During the growing (anagen) phase a hair on your
scalp grows at a rate of about one centimeter (0.4 inch)
a month, which is about 12 centimeters (5 inches) a
year, for between two and five years.

In the breaking-down (catagen) phase, the hair root

separates from the follicle and the lower half of the follicle degenerates. This takes a few weeks.

The separated old hair lies in the follicle in the resting (telogen) phase for about three months. It finally falls out in the phase called exogen.

Then the anagen phase starts again. The follicle regenerates and a new hair starts growing.

Adding it up

We have an average of 125,000 scalp hair follicles, depending on our type of hair. Each strand grows 12 centimeters (5 inches) per year, which is about the diameter of a CD. Just imagine 125,000 CDs lined up side by side. In a year, the total growth adds up to 15 kilometers, or 9 1/3 miles a year. That's about the same distance as 137 football fields—a long way for your hair to grow between one birthday and the next!

A tall story?

What about the story of Rapunzel,[4] the princess kept prisoner in a tower by a witch? Were her braids really long enough for the witch (and later the prince) to climb up and reach her?

Generally, uncut hair will grow to between 36 and 60 centimeters (1 or 2 feet). Some people can grow their hair as far as their shoulder blades, a few can grow it to their waist, but only one in a million can grow it to 1.5 metres (almost 5 feet), which is almost to their ankles. Still, towers are a lot taller than that, so Rapunzel was, well, unbelievable.

[4] You can read the story of Rapunzel in Grimms' fairy tales.

Dead and shed

Humans shed their hair constantly, unlike many animals that have definite molting seasons. Some animals grow thicker coats in winter for extra warmth, and then shed them as the warm weather approaches. A few animals, such as the Arctic fox, change the color of their coats—the brown summer coat is replaced by a white one for winter camouflage, and vice versa when spring returns.

When cats and rabbits lick themselves clean, they swallow the shedding hairs. Sometimes they swallow so many they develop hairballs that can block their intestines. A high-fiber diet and daily grooming to get rid of the loose hairs will help prevent this.

Chapter 4

Wear it, walk on it, work with it

See how many different things made from or containing hair or fur you can find in the description below. (The answer is on the page opposite, upside-down.) Do you know where each one comes from?

Imagine it's turned cold and you've hurried home to fetch something warmer to wear. You're covered with goosebumps. Brrrrrrr. You open the front door and step onto a rug in the hall. Great-granny is knitting by the fire. She has a mohair throw over her knees and is listening to your little brother practicing his violin.

Great-granny always wears a locket. Once she

opened it to show you a curl of hair from her daughter who died. She keeps Great-grandpa's shaving brush on her dressing table, too.

In your bedroom you pull open drawers, looking for your angora beret and scarf. Drat! Your sister must have borrowed them.

"Mo-o-o-m!"

Your mother's at her easel, painting. She takes you into her room and opens her wardrobe. Her camel-hair coat is hanging beside your father's best wool suit. When she lends you her cashmere cardigan, her alpaca scarf and her mink beret, you give her a hug. You notice her fleecy slippers beside the bed that's covered with woollen blankets.

Before dashing out again to join your friends, you brush your hair and put on some lipstick, blush and eye shadow. Now that you're warm, your goosebumps have disappeared.

Answer: Did you get 19?—floor rug, knitting, mohair throw, violin bow, locket hair, shaving brush, angora beret & scarf, paintbrush, camel-hair coat, wool suit, cashmere cardigan, alpaca scarf, mink beret, slippers, blankets, hairbrush, blush & eye shadow brushes—or 20 if you counted lipstick brush.

Fine fleeces and fashions

Here's where the items on pages 28–29 come from.

Sheep's wool Fine wool from merino sheep makes fashion garments. Coarser wool from other breeds is excellent for blankets, carpets and army uniforms. Unwoven wool (fleece) is used to line boots and for car seat covers.

Alpaca Alpacas are members of the camel family and come from South America. They are shorn once a year. Alpaca is used in clothes, blankets, carpets and duvets. It's super warm.

Camel hair Bactrian camels (the camels with two humps) live on the arid plains of Asia. They molt, so their tan hair can be gathered by hand and woven into camel hair coats and blankets.

Cashmere is luxuriously soft and light. It comes from Kashmir goats that live in the Himalayas. When these goats molt, people comb out the hair. In some countries, including Australia, New Zealand, Afghanistan and Iran, the goats are shorn.

Angora and mohair come from Angora rabbits and Angora goats. For hundreds of years people raised these animals in Angora, now called Ankara—the capital of Turkey.

Angora is a fine, luxury fiber that's spun into yarn for sweaters, berets and scarves as soft as clouds and almost as fluffy as the rabbits it comes from. The rabbits can be shorn every three months from the time they are two months old.

Mohair is a soft, hairy fiber, excellent at trapping heat, and very light. It comes from the long, silky coat of Angora goats, and is used for blankets and knitwear. The goats are shorn twice a year.

Mink are weasel-like, semiaquatic animals that live in Asia, Europe and North America. In the wild they make their homes in burrows. In Canada, the US and other countries they are farmed for their fur. The American mink was introduced into Britain in the 1920s to establish a fur trade, but some escaped and multiplied. Now in Britain they are treated as a pest because they destroy native wildlife. Mink fur is used to make coats, hats, muffs and decorative trim for clothing.

Horsehair for the bows of violins and other stringed instruments comes from the tails of specially bred horses in Mongolia, Siberia, China, Japan and Canada where it's cold and the food supply is limited. The horses suffer very little infection and illness, and as a result their hair grows finely and evenly. Only the best hair is used. It's washed, disinfected and sorted by hand into hanks that are sold to makers and repairers of stringed instruments. The bow for a violin contains approximately 160 hairs, depending on the type of horsehair.

In some countries, judges and barristers (lawyers who argue cases in the court room) wear wigs made of whitish horsehair.

Besides wearing horsehair, people once slept on it. Before bouncy inner springs were invented, horsehair was used to fill mattresses. These were made with a tough outer covering so they weren't too prickly.[5]

[5] But a few deeply religious people in the Middle Ages *wanted* to be prickled. They wore shirts lined with hair from the manes and tails of horses to punish themselves, as a penance for their sins.

Hog bristle is the stiff, coarse hair from pigs. It's used for hairbrushes and paintbrushes.

Brushes for oil painting are made from the hair of hog and sable (a weasel-like creature). Softer hair from camel, sable, squirrel, pony, badger, ox and mongoose is used for watercolor brushes.

Hair from squirrel, pony, sable, goat and raccoon is used for cosmetic brushes. Shaving brushes for lathering faces are made from badger hair.

In China, brush pens for painting and calligraphy are made from goat hair, angora, sable and many different creatures, including wolves and rats.

Ghosts, growls and goosebumps

When we're cold, goosebumps erupt over our skin. Spooky movies make our spines tingle. When a dog growls, the hair on its neck stands up. It's the same reaction each time. A hair-raising experience!

It works like this. A tiny muscle called the arrector pili is attached to every hair follicle. When we're frightened or angry, our body reacts instantly—it's a reflex.[6] The arrector pili automatically tightens,

---

[6] Reflexes are controlled by the autonomic nervous system, which is responsible for many automatic actions in our body, including heartbeat and digestion.

pulling each hair up straight. In animals the effect is very obvious—think of your cat when it sees a dog. Immediately it looks bigger and more fearsome.

Cold also prompts the arrector pili to tighten. As each hair rises, the skin around it is pulled up into a small bump—a goosebump. If you look closely you'll see a hair standing upright in the middle of each bump. The erect hairs insulate you against the cold by trapping warmth radiating from the body. We don't have enough hairs for this to help much, though. To make a real difference, we have to add animal hairs—put on a sweater.

Nothing but hair to make taxes fair

In England during the eleventh century, Earl Leofric promised his wife, Lady Godiva, that he'd reduce taxes on the poor people of Coventry if she rode naked from one end of the town to the other.

Some people say Godiva let down

35

her long hair to cover herself. There's a story that the only person in Coventry who looked at her was Tom the tailor. He was struck blind immediately. Ever since, people who steal looks through windows and keyholes at nude or undressing people have been called "peeping Toms."

Bristling about fur

For thousands of years, humans have worn furry animal skins. Australian Aborigines used possum and kangaroo skins, the Inuit have made clothing from sealskin to keep out the intense cold, and African chiefs have worn capes of leopardskin. All of them killed only what they needed.

Today coats, hats, earmuffs and soft toys are sometimes made from the fur of dogs, cats, rabbits, foxes, mink, beavers, seal pups and all sorts of other animals. Not long ago, people visited Asia to shoot tigers so they could take home a tigerskin rug.

Lots of animals, such as the tiger, have been hunted almost to extinction. Others, such as mink, dogs and cats, are often farmed and skinned in cruel conditions. Many people refuse to buy clothing or toys made of fur because of this.

Declare the hair

Whenever you enter Canada or the US you must declare what's in your luggage. Souvenirs such as soft toys, musical instruments or clothing made from skins, furs, wool or animal hair might be carrying a disease or insect that is not present in North America. If it is from an endangered species it may be confiscated. If the item is not from an endangered species you may be asked to prove to the quarantine officers that it is completely clean.

Chapter 5

Disappearing

Nuts about seeds

What would you think if your father began rubbing his head with a big bowlful of parsley seed every morning? You'd say he was nuts, wouldn't you?

In eighteenth-century England nobody would have thought that. Back then, parsley seed was recommended for preventing baldness.

If finding so much parsley seed was a problem,

A FAT LOT OF USE

More than 3500 years ago the Egyptians were just as troubled by baldness. The treatment they used for it is written on an ancient medical papyrus that's now in the University Library of Leipzig in Germany. Imagine hunting for these ingredients (mixed in equal quantities):

the fat of a lion, the fat of a hippopotamus, the fat of a crocodile, the fat of a cat, the fat of a snake, the fat of an ibex.

a balding man could mix together boars' grease (pig fat), the ashes of burnt bees, almond oil, lily-root oil and wormwood. Apparently, the best time to start applying this goo was the day before full moon.

The Romans loathed balding, too. Some painted their scalps to make it seem like they had hair.

Over 2000 years ago, Hippocrates (the "father of medicine") wrote that people who are bald don't have varicose veins, but if a bald person *does* develop varicose veins his hair will grow again. Can you find someone this has happened to . . . ?

Failing follicles

When we're born we have over
1000 hair follicles per square
centimeter on our scalp, or
6500 per square inch (about
125,000 total). As we grow
and our scalp stretches,
this reduces to about 200
follicles per square centimeter (or 1300 per square
inch). The existing hairs spread out. As we age, we
lose some—every ten years about 2000 follicles stop
producing hair. This doesn't mean we're all going bald,
but it does mean the thatch on our heads is slowly
getting thinner. When we're really old, lots of us (both
men and women) will be a bit thin on top.

Obvious bald patches occur when big hairs are shed
and then replaced by short, vellus-like hairs. Some
people take medication that slows down or stops the
balding process. Others have hair transplants, or wear
a wig or a patch of hair called a toupee, while others
leave their baldness on view for the rest of their lives.

Humans aren't the only creatures that go bald. Some other primates—orangutans, chimpanzees, gorillas and macaques—do, too.

Born to bald

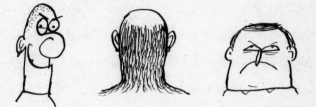

This is one time you really *can* blame your parents.

Men who go bald while they're still young almost always have bald fathers. Several genes, including one passed on by the mother, play a part in this. We know that the scalp follicles begin producing only the short, fine, colorless hair called vellus instead of long strands of normal hair.

Women also suffer from this sort of hair loss, although their hair tends to thin out. Only rarely do they develop really bald patches. Still, by the time they reach their eighties only about one woman in three will have kept all her hair.

Prince Edward of England and Prince Albert of Monaco might be royal, but they've both lost their crowning glory, thanks to their parents.

Bald and bothered

Another royal, Queen Marie Antoinette of France, probably suffered from a different type of balding called alopecia areata (allo-PEE-sha arry-AH-ta). This disease is extremely upsetting. People lose clumps of pigmented hair from their head and other parts of their body such as their eyelids and eyebrows. Usually the hair grows back. Marie Antoinette lost her head before her hair had a chance. She was sent to the guillotine and beheaded.

Bald and brave

Have you ever known anyone having treatment for cancer who went bald? People having chemotherapy and radiation often lose their hair, but it grows back once the therapies finish.

Some medications will also cause all hair on the body to fall out.

Bald and bugged

Common ringworm is a fungus that can cause bald patches in cats, dogs and humans. After you use the right cream or medication to kill the infection the follicles generally start producing hair again.

Bogus balding for brilliant results

There are people who *make* themselves bald.

Some men regularly shave off all their head hair to be fashionable, or to avoid being only partially bald. People call their shiny crowns "chrome domes," or "cue balls."

Many swimmers believe having no hair on their heads or bodies reduces water drag and therefore makes them faster. Before swim meets they "shave down."

Racing cyclists shave their legs. Some say it helps them ride faster. Others shave to avoid infection in case they fall, because hairs in a cut or gravel rash make it difficult to keep a wound clean. And they know that ripping a bandage off hairy skin *really* hurts.

Sometimes patients are shaved before an operation. The hair is removed from wherever the surgeon is going to make a cut, to avoid infection later.

Chapter 6

Head gear

We've been wearing wigs for
thousands of years. Upper-class Egyptians had them.
French and English nobles wore them 300 years ago.
In the seventeenth and eighteenth centuries, naval men
like Captain Cook wore wigs when they were at sea.
Some judges, opera singers, actors and ballet dancers
still clap on hairpieces as part of a day's work.

From bare to hair

No respectable ancient Egyptian man or woman would
dream of going to a social gathering without wearing
a wig. Many wore wigs every day. Lots shaved their

heads because it was a great way to stay free of lice. Besides, wearing a wig in Egypt was cooler and more comfortable if you were bald. The wigs were finely braided, or decorated with beads and gold thread. Some were buried with their owners for use in the afterlife.

At a party or festive occasion, an Egyptian woman wore a perfumed cone of fat and scent on top of her wig. Her body heat made the cone melt slowly so it trickled fragrantly over the wig down onto her skin.

People who didn't shave their heads wore hairpieces to extend their own hair and change their appearance, as some people still do today.

Big wigs for bigwigs

In seventeenth-century France people from all walks of life wore wigs. Poorer people wore cheap horsehair ones, while rich people wore expensive ones made of human hair.

Important and aristocratic people in England and France began

wearing bigger and
bigger wigs in the 1670s.
Fashionable women
had wigs that rose up
to a meter (3 1/4 feet) above
their heads. Men wore elaborately
curled wigs, long enough to cover their
shoulders. The English called them "periwigs,"
and eventually shortened the word to "wigs."

Staff in royal households included dozens of
wigmakers who created, restyled and cared for wigs.
Besides hair, wigmakers used padding and powder, fat,
and wads of wool for their coiffured creations that they
cooked rock-hard in ovens. The baked result
was a monstrous meringue of rolls and
curls. Into this the wigmaker attached
or threaded all sorts of adornments,
such as feathers, clocks, model ships
and jewelry. The woman's own hair was
woven into the lower part of the wig.
Finally the whole folly was anchored in
place with a variety of hairpins, from the

sharpened stick type to bent bobby pins.
It was a construction built to last . . . for weeks.

Women couldn't take off their wigs when
they went to sleep because they were so firmly fixed to
their heads. No one considered cleanliness. Mice crept
into the wigs to nest in the greasy padding that already
was alive with lice and other bugs. Little wonder some
women slept with mousetraps on their pillows!

Balancing such huge contraptions was not easy.
Ordinary people began to laugh at those who wore big
wigs, and soon dubbed them "bigwigs." We still use this
word for people in important positions, even though
they no longer wear such colossal headgear.

For real, for work, for fun

Modern wigmakers create wigs from human hair,
synthetic fiber or horsehair.

The best wigs are made from Caucasian virgin hair,
because it takes up color easily and holds a curled
or wavy style well. Virgin hair is hair that's never been
dyed or tinted. It doesn't matter if it's turning gray.

One of the best sources is men who decide to cut off their ponytails, because many of them have never colored their hair artificially.

Asian hair is black and straight and has to be bleached, tinted and permed if it's for a Caucasian-style wig. These processes damage Asian hair, making it harder to dye, as well as shortening its life. Asian hair is used a lot for hair extensions and curls in the theatre.

Judges in England and Australia wear large frizzy wigs made from horsehair. The wigs can be very old because they're sometimes handed down through families.

Why do judges wear wigs? It's partly due to tradition and it's supposed to create a solemn atmosphere in the courtroom. Wigs also help to make judges more anonymous in court during criminal trials.

Synthetic fiber is used for wigs in the entertainment and fashion industry, and for wigs that are needed for only a short time. They are the cheapest of all and come in every color of the rainbow, but they're hot to wear.

Keeping it on

Boys and girls who wear wigs can still play sports or hang upside-down on monkey bars. A special adhesive tape called toupee tape holds a wig in place. Once the hair starts to grow again, tiny clip-combs keep the wig firmly attached until it's no longer required.

Toupees and transplants

Toupees are patches of hair that wigmakers create for people who want to cover a bald area. They're kept in place with tape and tiny clips. Sometimes a dermatologist-surgeon transplants small plugs of hair into a bald spot for a person who doesn't want a toupee.

Wig-washing

Wigs, like regular hair, must be kept clean. Ones made
of human hair should be washed on a head-shaped
wooden block by a wigmaker every three weeks, after
the cotton cap has been dry-cleaned. Synthetic wig hair
is washed as little as possible because heat and combing
cause the strands to crinkle.

Buying and selling

Wigmakers buy hair by weight from anyone with a
good length for sale: you, hairdressers, or hair brokers.
In the Western world long hair is not as fashionable as
it once was, and Caucasian hair is expensive because it's
not so plentiful any more. That is why some wigmakers
travel to brokers in the United Kingdom and France
to purchase hair of the color, luster and fineness that
they need.

If you have braids or a long ponytail that you don't
want any more, you could make some pocket money . . .

HOW TO MAKE A WIG

Wigs are made completely by hand. Here are the steps:

1 Measure the person's head.

2 Cut and sew a cap of cotton netting to fit exactly, threading in a short piece of elastic for adjustments.

3 Attach the hairs to the cap with a knotting needle, an instrument that has a metal handle and a fine wire-like hook at the end, a bit like a dentist's probe.

4 Make the part. This can take up to two weeks because the hair has to be stitched to make it *look* like a scalp and not appear sewn. It's extremely fine and dainty work.

5 Call in the hairstylist to create the hairdo the person wants for their wig.

Chapter 7

Shells, shaving and shedding blood

How would you like to shave yourself with a shark's tooth, or a sharpened seashell, or a piece of flint? Cave paintings show us that's what people used in the Stone Age. It didn't take long for these shaving implements to get blunt, but they were fairly easy to replace . . . disposable razors aren't a modern invention.

Shaving and other ways of removing hair on men and women has been around for 30,000 years.

Blades from glass to gold

Some African tribes and the Aztecs of Mexico used blades of obsidian (volcanic glass). The Romans and Greeks used razors made of iron. Archaeologists have found razors of copper, bronze and gold in ancient burial sites in Denmark and India, and in Tutankhamen's tomb in Egypt. Some were elaborately engraved and kept in leather cases.

Annoying nicks

Whatever sort of blade people shaved with, they found it hard to avoid nicking themselves. In the 1700s a Frenchman, Jean-Jacques Perret, designed the first safety razor. A metal shield on one side of the long blade helped to guard the skin from accidental cuts, although it didn't always work.

Razor styles changed, but blades required frequent sharpening until King Camp Gillette (an American, but not a monarch) invented wafer-thin disposable steel blades just over 100 years ago. Millions sold, along with the safety razor he designed for them. Soon whiskers disappeared and clean-shaven faces became common.

Jacob Schick invented the first electric shaver. It went on sale in New York in 1931. Great! No more nicks. Your whiskers poke through holes in the shaver's shield, and are cut off by whirring blades that can't touch the skin. Battery razors, introduced in 1960, work the same way.

Women have also used razors made of all sorts of materials. Electric shavers for them arrived in the 1940s.

Smooth skin

Razors and blades aren't the only way people have removed hair. Over 2000 years ago, Greek women risked scorching themselves as they used lamps to singe off the hair on their legs. Hair-pluckers worked at the public baths in Rome where they removed hair from men's armpits. Yes, they yelled!

Roman women rubbed away the hairs on their legs with pumice stone, or waxed them, like Indian and Egyptian women. All of them plucked their eyebrows, and smeared on depilatory creams and sugar pastes, just as women do today. In Elizabethan England, high foreheads were fashionable, so women plucked and shaved the hair from their eyebrows and above their foreheads to give themselves "the look."

Electrolysis is a modern way of removing hair. An electric current is sent through a needle into each hair follicle to destroy the hair root. Laser hair removal uses pulses of light to get rid of hair.

Barbers and babble

Our word "barber" comes from the Latin word for beard: *barba.* Thousands of years ago barbers worked in Egypt, Mesopotamia (an area in the Middle East that includes modern Iraq), Greece, Rome and Asia. Some were employed in private households. Others set up their own barbershops in villages and towns. These soon became snip–chat–shave centers for locals who wanted to catch up on news and gossip, or who wanted to have serious discussions with learned friends.

Barbers were held in such high esteem that a statue was erected in Rome to commemorate the first one, a Greek, who arrived from Sicily around 300 BCE.[8]

Being shaved in Rome was a slow and sometimes painful business because no soap was used. Young Roman men held a party to celebrate their first shave when they turned 21.

Many Roman barbers worked on street corners, just as some Asian barbers work outdoors today. In Vietnam, barbers nail a mirror to a tree or a wall, set up a wooden chair in front of it, and wait for passersby to stop for a haircut.

---

[8] BCE: Before the Common Era, the non-Christian form of "BC" ("before Christ").

A bloody business

Monks were the doctors of the Dark Ages, from around 500 to 1100 CE.[9] They needed the help of barbers to treat people because barbers owned blades. One of the common treatments then for all sorts of illnesses was bloodletting (a risky procedure—if too much blood drained away, or if infection entered the cut, this treatment could kill instead of cure).

In the twelfth century the Church forbade monks, because they were ministers of God, from having anything to do with the deliberate letting of human blood. So the barbers, who'd been the monks' assistants, took over. For several hundred years barber-surgeons bled people, lanced boils, pulled out teeth, set fractured bones and tended wounds. And all the time they kept on shaving and snipping.

[9] CE: Common Era; the non-Christian form of "AD" (Anno Domini, which means "in the year of our Lord").

To advertise his shop, a barber-surgeon placed a painted red and white pole outside, with a basin fixed to its top. Red and white were the color of blood and bandages. The pole represented a rod that people held when they were being bled, and the basin represented the bowl used to catch the blood. Some people say the pole was painted only red and the barber dried his bandages on it. They believe the spiral of red and white was created as the bandages twirled about in the wind and wrapped themselves around the pole.

In the 1700s trained surgeons separated from the barber-surgeons and formed their own professional group. Although cutting hair and cutting bodies are two distinct occupations today, poles with candy-cane stripes are still seen on barbershops. A knob or ball at the pole's top is a reminder of the bowl for blood.

Off-the-wall music

In the 1500s and 1600s, music often floated out of barbershops. Stringed instruments such as the guitar and the lute hung on the walls for customers to take down and play while they waited. Some sang as they plucked.

In 1770 a Frenchman called Beaumarchais wrote a play about a barber, *The Barber of Seville*. In 1816 the Italian composer, Rossini, set the story to music. Figaro, the barber, helps his former employer, a count, win the hand of a young woman. Of course there's a shaving scene.

In America a new kind of music is believed to have started in barbershops in the 1800s. Men in a "barbershop quartet" sing in four harmonized parts, with no piano or instrumental accompaniment.

The demon barber

A modern musical, *Sweeney Todd*, has helped keep alive the story of a barber who many people think was one of the worst mass murderers in Britain. Sweeney Todd, often referred to as "the demon barber of Fleet Street," is said to have lived in the 1700s, but lots of people say he never existed. True or not, stories about this barber and his actions were so grisly they've lived on.

Sweeney Todd devised a cunning way to murder customers who were in the shop alone with him, and who unwisely let on they were carrying valuables.

Todd's shop was built above a labyrinth of underground vaults. He cut a revolving trapdoor into the floor and screwed two barber's chairs on to it, one above on view in the shop, and the other one upside-down underneath where it couldn't be seen.

When Sweeney Todd released the trapdoor latch, the chair with someone sitting in it would suddenly tip backwards, pitching the person onto the stone floor of the vaults below. As the chair and customer swung down, the empty chair beneath revolved up into the shop. Todd would quickly latch it into position before dashing downstairs to cut the throat of his customer if the man wasn't already dead from the fall.

Now for the *really* gruesome part. Besides pocketing the customer's watch or jewelry or money, Sweeney Todd is said to have cut up the body and taken it through the passageway of vaults to the underground kitchen of his partner in crime, Mrs. Lovett. And guess what meat Mrs. Lovett put into her tasty pies that she sold to the people of London from her bakery upstairs?

Chapter 8

Superstitions and super strong

A long time ago in Fiji, you might have felt like hiding when the Chief of Namosi's hair was long. To make sure nothing evil happened, he always ate a man when he had his hair cut.

Maoris in parts of New Zealand used to gather together on their most sacred day of the year to have their hair cut with an obsidian knife.

All sorts of customs and superstitions have surrounded hair. Some are still practiced, while others have disappeared.

Nonsense, notions and potions

Do you care what day of the week your hair is cut? In the 1600s, English people believed it was lucky to cut your hair on Monday, and unlucky to cut it on Friday or Saturday. By the mid-1800s they believed the best time for cutting was when the moon was waning (becoming smaller). The hair was swept up immediately and burnt because people believed if a magpie pecked up some to line its nest, the person whose head it came from would die within a year.

Would you comb your hair at night if you had friends or relations at sea? In Scotland as recently as the 1930s some women refused to comb their hair at night if they did. Maybe it had something to do with waves . . .

If you wanted to cure a sty (an infection of the eyelid) would you wait until the full moon, take one hair from the tail of a black cat, and rub it nine times across the infection? That's what English people did in the 1700s and 1800s. At around the same time the

Irish would take nine hairs from the tail of a black cat, chop them up, soak them in water and then drink the mixture to relieve whooping cough.

Boys and girls were once told to eat the crusts of bread to make their hair grow curly. Perhaps that was because people with curly hair were said to be good-natured. People with straight hair were thought to be cunning.

Redheads had plenty to worry about back in the 1500s. In those days people said they must be witches, and burnt them at the stake. Beliefs changed and later on some people thought it was lucky to run their fingers through a person's red hair.

People have wished on eyelashes since the 1800s. When an eyelash falls out you put it on the tip of a finger, blow it away and make a wish. If the eyelash stays stuck to the finger, though, the wish won't come true—or so people say.

The hairy business of staying strong

Three thousand years ago a judge called Samson lived in Israel. He had long hair and was so strong he could tear a young lion to pieces with his bare hands. Once, using the jawbone of a donkey, he killed 1000 men from the ancient country of Philistia.

When Samson fell in love with a woman called Delilah, the Philistines promised her loads of silver if she could persuade Samson to tell her the secret of his strength.

Delilah pestered. Eventually Samson revealed that an angel had visited his pregnant mother and instructed her never to cut her baby's hair.

Delilah lulled Samson to sleep and beckoned a man to cut off the sleeping judge's hair. Then the Philistines captured Samson easily, because his strength had vanished. They gouged out his eyes and set him to work grinding grain in prison. But week after week his hair grew back.

The Philistines decided to make their blind prize prisoner fight others who could see. Thousands of people gathered inside the temple and on its roof to watch. Samson asked the boy who led him into the temple to place him where he could feel two pillars and lean against them. Here was his chance for revenge, although he knew it meant his own death. Samson put his arms around the two pillars that supported the temple, and pulled them down. The roof, masonry and spectators came crashing down onto everyone, and thousands of people died.

Chapter 9

The long and short of hair

Suppose it was your hairstyle, instead of a ring on your finger, that told people if you were married. The Kirghiz are a nomadic people who live in central western Asia. Kirghiz girls braid their hair in lots of thin braids, but after they marry they wear their hair in only two.

If you're a boy, imagine waiting years for your first haircut. In the Cook Islands a feast is prepared to celebrate it.

Your hair is divided and tied into the same number of locks as the number of guests, and each guest is given a lock as a memento.

Our hair is hugely important to each of us, whether we keep it, display it, hide it or shave it off. Some religions and cults have rules about it based on the teaching of their prophets or founders.

Devoted followers

Sikhism began in India in the sixteenth century. Sikhs never cut any hair because uncut hair is one of their five sacred symbols for living in harmony with the will of God. Boys gather their hair into a topknot and cover it with a square of cloth called a *rumal*, and men wrap their hair in a turban. Women cover their hair.

Buddhist monks shave their heads and don't wear beards as a sign of submission to Buddha, the religious leader who lived in India in the sixth century BCE.

Hasidic Jewish men follow an instruction about hair in Leviticus, one of the books in the Jewish Torah that is also in the Old Testament. They wear long curls of hair in front of their ears because they are not allowed to cut the corners of their beards. Some orthodox Jewish women cover their hair with a *sheitel* (wig) or a scarf or hat for modesty when they go out.

In public, Muslim women cover their hair with scarves, also for modesty, according to the laws of their religion. Muslim men keep their moustaches or beards well-trimmed.

Dreadlocks are long, twisted ropes of hair worn by Rastafarians, followers of a Jamaican cult named after Ras Tafari. Ras Tafari is the former name of Haile Selassie, emperor of Ethiopia 1930–36 and 1941–47.

Off with it!

Over 2000 years ago the Macedonian king, Alexander the Great, thought it would be easy for the enemy to grab hold of a soldier's beard with one hand and slit his throat with a dagger in the other. So Alexander made his soldiers go into battle clean-shaven.

The Manchus who conquered China in the seventeenth century insisted the Chinese men, the

Hans, wear the Manchu hairstyle: a partly shaven head with the remaining hair braided into a long braid. This was a kind of protective camouflage—making it harder to tell the hated conquerors, the Manchus, from the Hans. Any Hans who refused to adopt the style were killed. Men wore single braids until the 1920s.

Elvis Presley grew a quiff, a curl of hair over the forehead. It was cut off when he joined the US Army and had the regulation crewcut.

Billygoats and queens

It's not only men and billygoats that have beards. Queens in ancient Egypt tied on artificial beards as a symbol of their regal position. It made them appear more like a male pharaoh!

Czar Peter the Great reformed Russia's army and navy during his reign from 1682 to 1725. To pay for these improvements he introduced taxes on thousands of items, including beards.

Different kinds of beards are often given names. The smallest beard is the goatee—really a tuft in the middle of the chin. The short and pointy "Vandyke beard" is named after the Flemish painter, Sir Anthony Vandyke. A full beard covers the upper lip, cheeks and chin, while an "old-man's beard" mightn't be a beard at all because it's also the common name of clematis, a plant that bears fluffy, hair-like fruit.

Dead head

Some people say beards grow on men after they die. Spooky! But the whiskers do *not* grow. After a person dies the body dehydrates (dries out). The skin on the face shrinks back and exposes the whiskers that were just below the skin's surface.

Something on the side

General Burnside, a soldier who fought in the American Civil War of 1861–65, grew whiskers down in front of his ears and kept them to the side of his face. The style caught on. Somehow the general's name was turned around and the new fashion became known as "sideburns."

Muttonchop whiskers, as the name suggests, are shaved to the shape of chops on the cheeks. They were popular in the 1800s.

A bit of lip

Like beards, moustaches are often named after their shape. A **pencil** mustache is a thin growth across the upper lip. Some military people wear **toothbrush** mustaches that are rectangular and immaculately trimmed—like a new toothbrush, not a squashed-out, used one.

Mark Twain, the American novelist and humorist, had a **walrus** mustache.

It drooped past either side of his mouth, halfway to his chin. A **handlebar** mustache is thick and has both ends waxed and twisted to fine points curling up at either side. People smile when they see one, like the mustache itself. Adolf Hitler, the Nazi dictator of Germany, grew a tiny square mustache the width of his nostrils. It became known as a **Hitler** mustache, but now the man is so despised you rarely see that style.

From wind to motors

Hairdressing salons for women first appeared toward the end of the 1800s.

Antoine, a French hairdresser, saw women with their long hair exposed to the wind and rain as they rode in Henry Ford's new invention, the motor car, early in the 1900s. "They need short hair," he thought —and the bob was born. This hairstyle reached just below the ears, and could be worn smooth and sleek, or with waves and curls.

Small electrical motors revolutionized women's hairdressing. It started with the vacuum cleaner. Vacuums sucked up the dirt at one end and blew out hot air at the other. It wasn't long before women took advantage of this. Previously they'd dried their hair in the sun and the wind. The first proper electrical hair dryer was developed in Germany in the 1920s, and by the 1950s handheld models were light and safe enough to be used in homes.

Shocking!

The ancient Egyptians and Greeks wound their hair around heated tongs to produce temporary curls, ringlets and waves on their heads and beards. These days women use electric curling irons.

Permanent waving, or "perm" for short, was introduced early in the twentieth century. It uses chemical solutions that alter the structure of hair strands to create waves and curls. The look lasts until the permed hair is either cut off or grows out.

The early perms were risky. A woman could be electrocuted as rods with her hair wound around them were individually wired up to an electrical machine. Some women suffered burns from the rods or from the steam that at times was part of the perming process.

Today a cold-wave method is used to perm hair. Chemical solutions are applied cold, or with only mild heat. Other cold chemical solutions are used to straighten curly or frizzy hair, a sort of reverse permanent wave.

A passion for fashion

Some styles hang around for years, while others disappear quickly. Crewcuts were probably first worn by the rowing crews at Yale and Harvard universities in the eastern states in the 1940s. They are still common. But the "beehive" style of the 1960s is rarely seen now. Women sprayed their hair cardboard-stiff to keep the beehive shape.

Many African girls wear their hair in tightly braided thin "cornrows." The Afro hairstyle of long, tight curls trimmed into a large round ball is a unisex cut seen in many countries.

The Mohawk got its name from its supposed similarity to an Iroquois hairstyle. The scalp is shaved except for a strip of hair that stands up from the neck to the forehead.

Punk hairstyles originated in the 1970s when punk rock was the rage. The brightly colored spikes of hair attract everyone's attention.

A bun is a twisted coil of hair wound and pinned into the shape of a round roll at the back of the head. Ballet dancers often keep their hair neat this way on stage.

Cutting hair doesn't hurt us because the strands we see are dead and have no nerves. But pulling on hair *does* hurt because there are nerves in the skin surrounding the follicles.

Signs and logos can be shaved into the back of heads. Mousses and gels help keep styles in place, while all colors of the rainbow in pastel and outrageous hues are available.

Chapter 10

A hairy story
by Red Blackhead

On Saturday my
father took us to
his office picnic
at the top of
Mount Curlytop.
The shortcut to
the peak of the
mountain has lots
of hairpin bends.

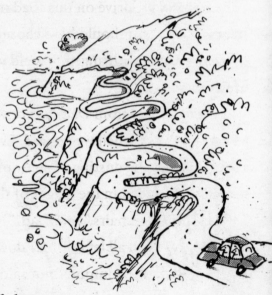

We had a couple of close
shaves on the way and missed going over the edge
by a whisker, but Dad didn't turn a hair.

"Whose hairbrained suggestion was it to come up here for a picnic?" my sister whined. She complains about everything. It's enough to make you tear your hair out.

"Mine," said Dad. He's a bigwig in his company.

"Trust you to have such a lousy idea," said my sister.

Dad told her not to wig out.

A car swerved in front of us and Mum gasped. "The way people drive on this road makes my hair stand on end. You should have chosen a safer place."

Dad bristled with anger. "Would you both get out of my hair?"

Lots of people from Dad's office were already at Mount Curlytop when we arrived. Everyone was arguing about whether the dusting of snow on the pinnacle should be included in the height of the mountain.

"Let's not split hairs," said Dad. "Now that we're away from work we can all let our hair down."

"Hey, Red," the computer nut said to me. "Have some chili with hot sauce. It'll put hair on your chest."

Yuk.

Hairy can mean dangerous, frightening, risk-taking.

Red and **Carrottop** are nicknames used for someone who has red hair.

Hairpin bends are narrow U-shaped bends, like hairpins.

Close shaves are near misses or narrow escapes. The expression comes from the fine distance involved in shaving closely without nicking the skin so that it bleeds.

A **whisker** (sometimes also called a **hair's breadth**) means a tiny distance. A hair is approximately 0.03 mm (0.001 inch) thick.

To not turn a hair is to stay calm without showing annoyance or distress. It's the opposite of both bristling with anger and having your hair stand on end (see opposite).

Hairbrained is sometimes spelt harebrained which is closer to its origin as it relates to hares. When male hares fight each other for females they become wild and excitable—in other words, a little crazy.

To tear your hair out comes from ancient times. When people were very upset and mourning the loss of a loved one, they tore at their hair.

A **bigwig** is an important person. The term started in the seventeenth century when noble or important people in England and France wore enormous wigs.

Lousy literally means infected with lice. Having lice in your hair can be unpleasant, and the word has acquired that meaning.

To wig out means to overreact or to become deliriously excited.

Make my hair stand on end This is the arrector pili at work (see pages 34–35). Our hairs literally stand up when we're scared, cold or angry, like a dog's hackles.

To bristle with anger also originates from the hairs on a dog's neck rising when it's annoyed.

To get out of someone's hair means to stop annoying them.

To split hairs is to squabble about petty differences. It is possible to literally split a hair, but does it make much difference to anyone except a scientist or dermatologist?

To let your hair down means to have an enjoyable and relaxing time. In the past, women with long hair always wore it pinned up if they went out or when they received visitors. Only at home and in private did they let it down.

To put hair on your chest means to make you a stronger person or more grown up.

Glossary

alopecia areata an autoimmune disease resulting in baldness

anagen the growing phase in the life cycle of a hair

arrector pili tiny muscle attached to a hair follicle

catagen the breaking-down phase in the life cycle of a hair

coiffure a person's hairstyle

dermatologist a medical specialist who treats people for skin and hair problems

dermis the layer of skin beneath the epidermis, containing hair follicles, oil glands, arrector pili, nerves and sweat ducts

DNA deoxyribonucleic acid, present in every person's cells and showing their genetic makeup

epidermis the outer layer of skin

eumelanin pigment that colors hair black or brown

exogen the shedding phase in the life cycle of a hair

follicle indentation of the skin from which a hair grows

hair extension a tress of long hair worn to extend a person's own hair

keratin tough protein forming the main part of hair, nails, hooves, horn and feathers

lanugo colorless hair on a baby in the womb, lost a few weeks before birth at full term

melanin pigment that colors skin and hair

perm, permanent wave the application of chemicals to hair to create waves and curls that will last for months

periwig an extremely large wig

pheomelanin pigment that colours hair blond or red

subcutaneous fat the layer of fat and capillaries beneath the skin

sugaring the application of sugar paste to remove unwanted hair

telogen the resting phase in the life cycle of a hair

terminal hair coarse, colored hair —we're born with some and some emerges at puberty

toupee a hairpiece worn to cover a bald patch

vellus hair short, fine, almost invisible hair seen on the faces of young children and women, and sometimes on men's bald heads

virgin hair hair that has never been dyed or tinted

Where to find out more

Books

K. L. Badt, *Hair There and Everywhere*, Children's Press, Chicago, 1994

Lionel Bender, *Forensic Detection*, Gloucester Press, New York, 1990

P. Haining, *Sweeney Todd: The Real Story of the Demon Barber of Fleet Street*, Boxtree Ltd, London, 1993

J. Levy, *Really Useful: The Origin of Everyday Things*, Willowdale, Firefly Books, 2002

I. Opie and M. Tatem, eds, *A Dictionary of Superstitions*, OUP, New York, 2005

David Owen, *Police Lab*, Willowdale, Firefly Books, 2002

B. Weider and D. Hapgood, *The Murder of Napoleon*, Congdon & Lattes, London, 1982

B. Weider and S. Forshufvud, *Assassination at St. Helena Revisited*, revised edition, John Wiley and Sons Inc., New York, 1995

Websites

Thousands of Internet sites have information on hair. They may differ from each other—perhaps some aren't up-to-date with the latest research, or they are trying to sell a product, or professional opinions vary. Here are a few.

- Young Forensic Scientists Forum at www.aafs.org/yfsf/index.htm
- The United States National Library of Medicine at www.nlm.nih.gov
- The Worshipful Company of Barbers at www.barberscompany.org.uk/indexb.html
  Click on "history"
- Some schools have Crazy Hair Day photos on their websites
- www.worldbeardchampionships.com

Index

About the author and illustrator

DIANA LAWRENSON was teased at school, because her thick hair stuck out. She hated it, just as her sister hated having red curly hair. When Diana was in her twenties her hair began to go gray, and now she wonders if there's more "gray matter" outside her head than in.

Diana trained as a nurse and has worked in hospitals in Australia, England and the Solomon Islands, where she encountered cyclones, earthquakes and crocodiles. Diana's other books are: *Pickle the Perfectly Awful Pig*, *Inside the Australian Ballet* (CBC Honour Book 2000) and *Guide Dogs: From Puppies to Partners* (CBC-shortlisted 2002).

LEIGH HOBBS is an artist and author best known for his children's-book characters Old Tom and Horrible Harriet. *Horrible Harriet* was shortlisted for the 2002 CBC Picture Book of the Year award, as was *Old Tom's Holiday* in 2003. Leigh is currently working on the sequel to *Horrible Harriet*, having recently given birth to a new character called Fiona the Pig. His website is www.leighhobbs.com.

Thanks

I'd have been in a tangle without the help of many people who contributed their expertise to this book. Not one of them told me to get knotted. My grateful thanks go to dermatologist Associate Professor Rod Sinclair; molecular biologist Dr. Bentley Atchison and forensic toxicologist Dr. Jim Gerostamoulos of the Victorian Institute of Forensic Medicine; wigmakers Andrew and Rhonda Barnett; violinist Hilary Blackshaw; Sea World education coordinator Robert Landman; librarians Jude Mahoney of Cabrini Hospital and Rosalind Olsen of Monash University; Peter Morant of the Australian Quarantine and Inspection Service; hairdresser Helen Picciotto; alpaca breeder Bob Richardson; artist Ian Rogers; Elise Sullivan of the Victoria Police; the Alfred Hospital library; the University of Melbourne Veterinary Clinic and Hospital; staff at the Victorian Forensic Science Centre; and others who clarified information or made suggestions that sent me along dozens of enlightening and funny paths.

Diana Lawrenson

The publishers would like to thank the following for photographs used in the text: the Honey-Clarke family (pages 14–15), Kevin Russ/istockphoto.com and Bonnie Jacobs/istockphoto.com (page 14), students at Gordon West Public School (pages 16–17), Kyle Parsons and FireLight Films (pages i, 74), Lee Stranahan/istockphoto.com (page 78, top) Jocelyn Banyard (page 78, bottom right), George Dabrowski and Dave Anderson (page 78, bottom left).